PEOPLE WHO
HELP
US

Ambulance

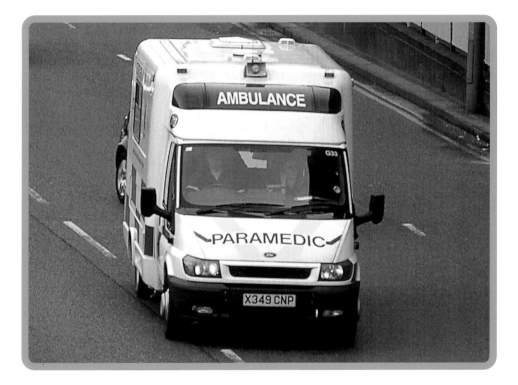

Clare Oliver

Photographs: Chris Fairclough

W
FRANKLIN WATTS
LONDON•SYDNEY

First published in 2002 by
Franklin Watts
96 Leonard Street
London
EC2A 4XD

Franklin Watts Australia
45–51 Huntley Street
Alexandria
NSW 2015

A CIP catalogue record for this book is available
from the British Library.

ISBN 0 7496 4670 5
Dewey Decimal Classification Number 362.1

Series Editor: Jackie Hamley
Cover Design: Peter Scoulding
Design: Sally Boothroyd

Photos
All commissioned photographs by Chris Fairclough.
The publishers would like to thank the following
for permission to use photographs:
www.shoutpictures.com 9
WMAS 14, 20, 21, 22, 23 (PTS team), 24 (Rachael), 25 (Rookie)
Newspix 26
St. John Ambulance 27

The author and publisher would especially like to thank the
West Midlands ambulance service for giving their help and time.

Printed in Malaysia

Contents

The ambulance service helps people in medical emergencies.

Paramedics and **technicians** go to help seriously ill or injured people. They use **first aid** to treat the illness or injury as soon as possible. They also take **patients** to hospital. Ambulance workers work in **shifts** so there is always a team ready to help.

The snake and staff (stick) in the middle of the crest are the symbols of Asclepius, the Ancient Greek god of healing.

CARL
TECHNICIAN

Paramedics and technicians often have their names sewn onto their shirts.

In this book, you will meet ambulance
workers from the West Midlands.
There are over 1,000 people in the team.
Here are just a few of them.

1 Rob   6 Jo
2 Dirk   7 Carl
3 Dave   8 Claire
4 Mandy   9 Chris
5 Geoff

Saving lives

■ **Teams of ambulance workers are saving lives right now.**

Ambulances are usually crewed by one paramedic and one technician. Paramedics have more training than technicians, but they both know how to use first aid and give emergency **medical** help.

Paramedics are not doctors but they are trained to give patients life-saving drugs.

Technicians use a **dummy** when they learn to **resuscitate** patients (restart their breathing).

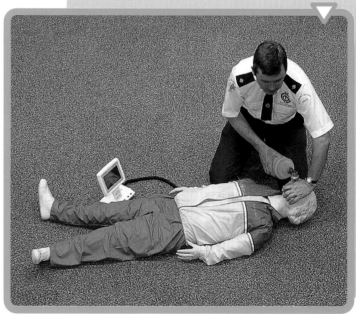

Ambulance crews help at all kinds of medical emergencies. It can be an illness, such as a heart attack or asthma attack, or it can be an accident, such as a fire.

The ambulance service sometimes teams up with other people to help us, for example the police and firefighters. All three services are usually needed when there is a traffic accident.

FACT

▷ *The UK ambulance service answers more than three million emergency calls a year.*

▷ *In just one year, the West Midlands ambulance service answers over 350,000 emergency calls.*

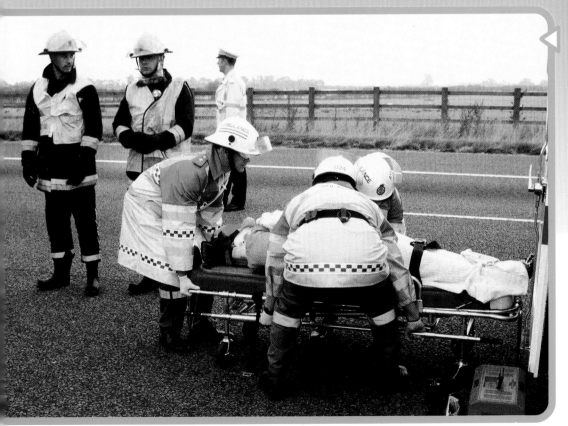

Ambulance workers, police and firefighters work together to help a man who has had a car accident.

Emergency!

In an emergency, someone calls for the ambulance service.

The calls are put through to the ambulance service's Emergency Operations Centre (**EOC**).

This is the EOC for the West Midlands ambulance service.

Helen is an EOC operator. She zooms into the map on her computer to find the caller's address and to choose the nearest ambulance.

The EOC operators find out where the emergency is. Then they ask about what has happened, and give advice on how to help the patient before the ambulance arrives. They send the information on to the ambulance crews.

FACT

▷ EOC operators use maps on their computers that show the position of every ambulance service vehicle. This is possible because the ambulances are tracked by satellite.

The operator sends information given by the caller on to a screen inside the ambulance.

Off to the emergency! ▷

AMBULANCE

PARAMEDIC

X349 CNP

Rapid response

When an ambulance is needed urgently, "first responders" are sent to the emergency.

First responders are paramedics in cars or on motorbikes who wait at special **standby points**. Their vehicles are good at getting through busy traffic. Ambulances also wait in different places around the area so they can reach emergencies quickly.

△ Billy's on standby, ready to help in the city centre.

Flashing blue lights and noisy sirens warn other traffic to move aside.

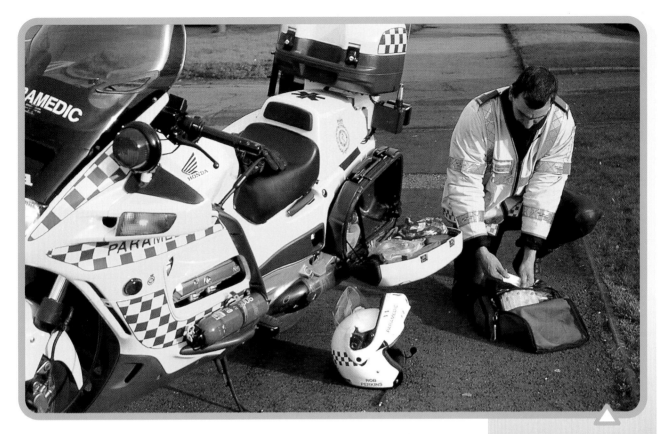

All the first aid equipment packs neatly into the side of Rob's motorbike.

First responders cannot take patients to hospital, but they can help them before an ambulance arrives. This can mean the difference between life and death. The quicker the patients receive first aid, the more likely they are to recover.

"
I always wanted to be a paramedic. How many other jobs can you leave at the end of the day knowing that you've made a real difference – that you've saved people's lives?
Rob, motorbike paramedic
"

First aid

▪ **The ambulance crew's first job is to make sure the patient's illness or injury does not get any worse.**

FACT

▶ *Technicians have three months of training before they go out in ambulances. They are not fully qualified until they have been in the job for a year.*

▶ *Only experienced technicians can train to be paramedics. Paramedics spend two months on special courses, including work in a hospital. They must go on a course every three years to update their skills.*

On arrival, paramedics and technicians might have to resuscitate a patient, stop any bleeding, put broken legs in **splints** – or even deliver a baby!

A first responder paramedic treats this cyclist's broken arm.

This patient is having trouble breathing, so Billy gives her an oxygen mask.

Paramedics and technicians wear **latex** gloves to avoid spreading or catching germs.

When the patient's condition is **stable**, the ambulance crew will usually take him or her to hospital for more medical help.

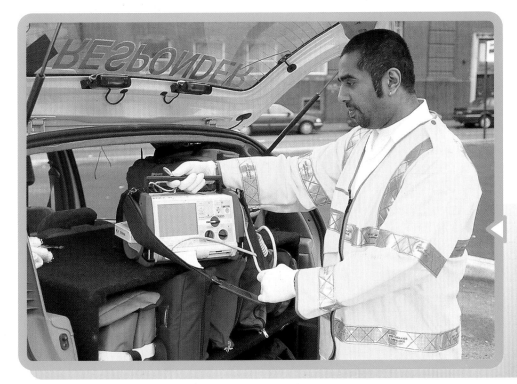

All the cars carry a **defibrillator**, a machine used to restart the heart.

On-board equipment

The ambulance service's motorbikes, cars and ambulances carry lots of equipment to help save lives.

Tim checks each item in the ambulance.

Some large items, such as stretchers, are only carried by ambulances. Each piece of equipment is checked at the start of each shift and after each **shout**.

No one knows what the next emergency will be, so it is very important that nothing is missing.

Ambulance crews visit the store room at the ambulance station for fresh **syringes**, bandages and other items.

> *Unless an ambulance has been checked, it's not ready for action. There's no point turning up to an emergency where a patient's not breathing and finding you've run out of oxygen.*
>
> **Ameta, paramedic**

Some of the important equipment carried by an ambulance.

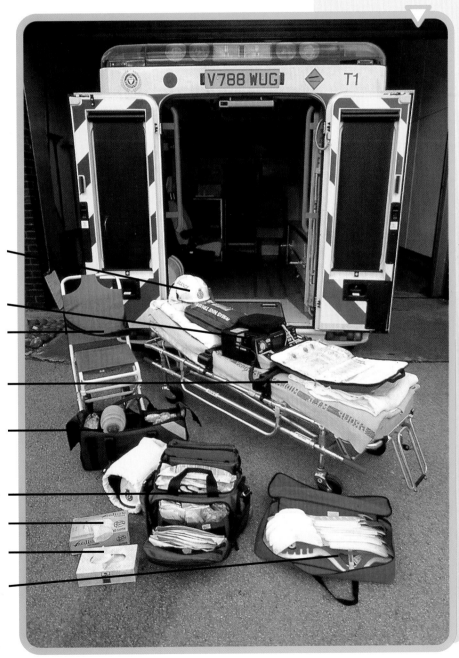

hard hat

defibrillator
(to restart the heart)

foldaway
wheelchair

stretcher

oxygen equipment
(to help with breathing)

paramedic's
bag

latex gloves

tissues

neck collars
(to support the
head and neck)

To hospital

In an emergency shout, the patient can only travel to hospital in an ambulance.

The paramedic decides which hospital to take the patient to, depending on which is nearest or can give the best care.

FACT

▷ Ambulances usually take emergency patients to **A&E**, the Accident and Emergency department of the hospital.

If the patient is able to talk, they are asked some questions in the ambulance.

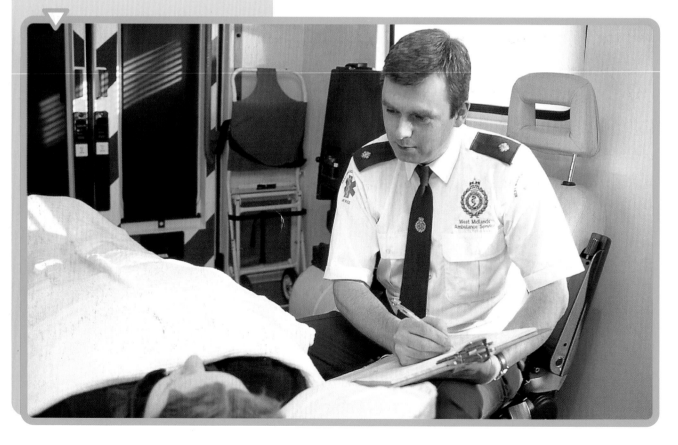

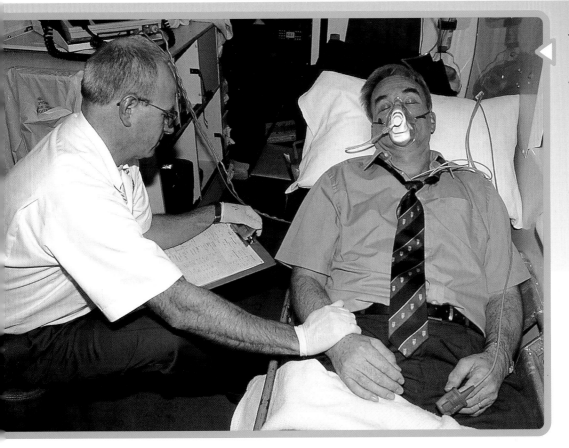

This patient has a problem with his heart. Les has hooked him up to the **ECG machine** in the ambulance.

In serious cases, the ambulance crew calls the hospital before they arrive. They can even send **data** about the patient straight into the hospital's computers. This means that hospital staff can be ready and waiting at the door to help the patient as soon as the ambulance arrives.

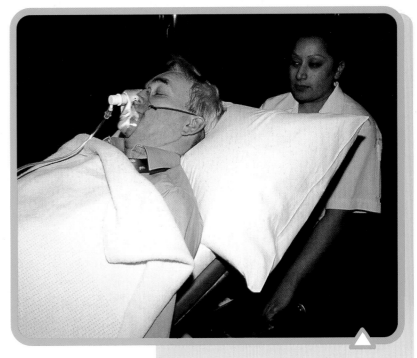

Ameta helps carry the patient into A&E for treatment.

Air ambulance

▓ For some emergencies, the air ambulance has to be called out.

The air ambulance helicopter is very useful when help is needed in places that are difficult to reach, or where there is a lot of traffic.

The air ambulance can cover distances very quickly.

FACT

▷ The West Midlands ambulance service shares its three air ambulances with eight other counties.

▷ These air ambulances look after nearly eight million people.

▷ On average, an air ambulance makes five journeys a day.

Each air ambulance helicopter carries two paramedics.

If someone is seriously injured on a hillside or hurt in a motorway crash, the air ambulance can get there first. Then it can fly the patient to a fully-equipped city hospital in a matter of minutes.

The air ambulance was able to reach this patient quickly, even though the accident was a long way from the nearest road.

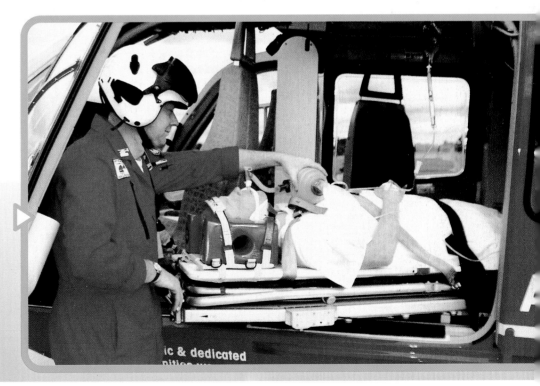

Emergencies are just one part of the ambulance service's work. The service also helps in other ways.

Their Patient Transport Service (PTS) vehicles take patients to **day care centres**, clinics and hospitals. The PTS vehicles are driven by ambulance care workers – people with special training in how to move patients and use first aid.

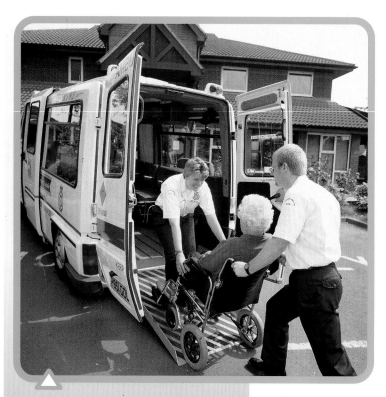

PTS vehicles have ramps at the back for wheelchairs.

FACT

▷ There are 8,000 non-emergency ambulance workers in the UK.

▷ On average, West Midlands PTS vehicles make over 5,000 patient journeys a day.

▷ The number for the patient advice service, called NHS Direct, is: 08 45 46 47.

▷ The West Midlands NHS Direct nurses answer a call every two minutes.

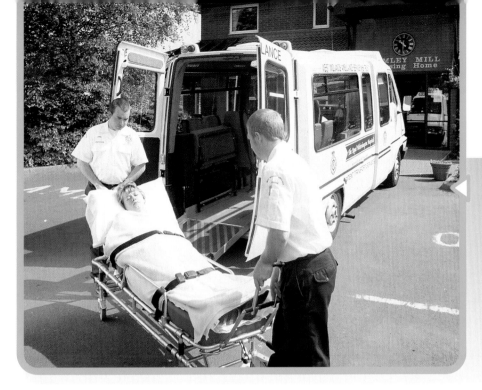

This woman is being taken to a hospital day appointment. Without the PTS teams to help her, she would have to stay in hospital all the time.

The ambulance service also helps people by giving advice. In the West Midlands, there are teams of NHS Direct nurses at the Emergency Operations Centre. They give medical advice to patients over the phone. If a call seems to be an emergency, the nurses can transfer it to the EOC operators.

Heather's advice means that patients or their carers can deal with many situations at home.

Helping us help them

Ambulance workers teach people first aid.

Technicians and paramedics visit schools and youth groups, for example, to teach people what to do in an emergency and how to use first aid. One day, these skills may keep someone alive until an ambulance comes.

Dinner lady Jo is the model as Dave shows a class of children how to put a broken arm in a sling.

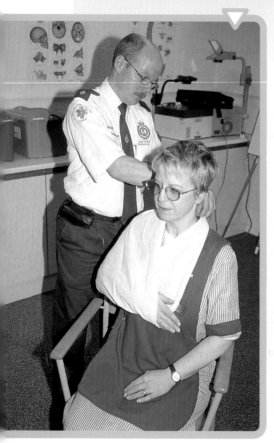

Rachael helped her mum when she fell ill and received an award for her bravey.

> *We give out bravery awards to members of the public who help save someone's life. We want to show how people can help us.*
> **Chris, education officer**

The West Midlands ambulance service has a website. The website has information about jobs, NHS Direct, raising money for the air ambulance and many other things.

Everyone can help the ambulance service. One way is to raise money for special services, such as the air ambulance.

There are even local clubs that you can join to learn life-saving skills and first aid. In the West Midlands, there is a club called the "Rookies". Find out more about clubs where you live from your local library.

Another important way to help the ambulance service is to only ever dial for an ambulance in an emergency. A **hoax** call can cost someone else their life.

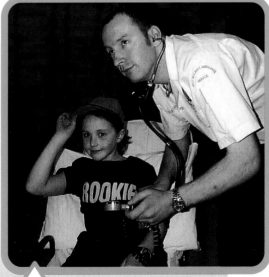

Paramedic Ian shows a Rookie how to take her blood pressure.

Help in action

Many lives are saved every day by ambulance services around the world.

The emergencies faced by ambulance workers depend on where they are. In places where there are wars, ambulance crews treat bomb victims or people with gunshot wounds, for example.

In some places, dangerous snake bites, spider bites or even jellyfish stings might be common. Whatever the situation, there is someone on hand to give emergency medical help.

Australian ambulance workers help a surfer who has been stung by a dangerous box jellyfish.

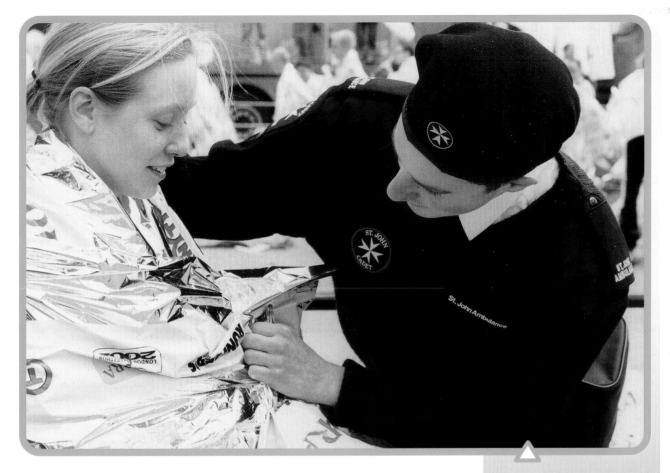

A St. John Ambulance cadet helps a runner after the London Marathon.

Some ambulance helpers are **volunteers**. St. John Ambulance, for example, has members all over the world. Its volunteers provide first aid cover at lots of public events. They also help the ambulance service by providing support in times of serious emergency.

St. John Ambulance has youth groups called Badgers and Cadets. These groups teach young people basic first aid and many other skills. See page 30 to find out how to become a member of one of these clubs.

Caring for Life

Keeping safe

- Never play in the road, and take care crossing the road.

- Always wear your seat belt when you're travelling in a car or coach.

- Take care when you get out of a car or bus and always get out on the pavement side.

- If you have asthma, remember to carry your inhaler. If you are diabetic, remember your treatment.

IN AN EMERGENCY

1. Never move a patient unless they are in danger (for example in a crashed car that may catch fire).

2. Check that there is nothing in a patient's airway (their mouth and throat) which might stop them breathing.

3. Don't crowd around someone who is ill. Give them space.

4. Reassure the patient while you wait for the ambulance. Hold their hand and talk in a soft, comforting voice.

5. Dial 999 and ask for an ambulance.

DIALLING 999

Dial 000 in Australia.

Only dial 999 in a real emergency. Be ready to:

1. Ask for the emergency service you need, for example "Ambulance".

2. Give the number of the telephone you're calling from and your name.

3. Say exactly where you are and what has happened.

4. Stay on the line until the operator says you can hang up.

Don't worry about answering lots of questions. The ambulance will already be on its way.

Glossary

A&E (Accident and Emergency) The department of a hospital that treats emergency cases.

data Information.

day care centre A place where people can go during the day to receive medical attention.

defibrillator A machine that uses an electric current to restart the heart.

dummy A pretend model of a person.

ECG machine A machine that can take pictures of the heart.

EOC (Emergency Operations Centre) The place where emergency calls for the ambulance service are taken.

first aid Treating the sick or injured before a doctor arrives or the patient gets to hospital.

first responder A paramedic who drives a car or a motorbike and who can reach an emergency quickly.

hoax Fake or joke.

latex Very thin rubber.

medical To do with medicine (treating ill and injured people).

paramedic The most highly trained type of emergency ambulance worker.

patient A person receiving treatment for an illness or injury.

resuscitate Start someone breathing again.

shift A period of work, planned so there is always someone working.

shout A call to attend an emergency.

splint A straight piece of wood or metal that is tied to a broken leg or arm to stop it from moving.

standby point A place where emergency vehicles wait for the next call.

syringe Used to inject drugs into a patient's body.

stable Not likely to get worse.

technician An emergency ambulance worker.

volunteer Someone who offers his or her time for free.

Further information

To find out more about the West Midlands ambulance service, visit: www.wmas.org

To find out more about the UK ambulance service and how to become an ambulance worker, visit: www.ambex.co.uk

In Australia, each state has its own ambulance service. Each service has a website that you can visit to find out more about the work they do.

To join Badgers or Cadets, the St. John Ambulance youth groups, visit:

www.sja.org.uk/young_people

or call: 08700 10 49 50

Index